The Call is His

by
Pastor Bill Newton

PUBLISH
AMERICA

PublishAmerica
Baltimore

ISBN: 1-4137-8331-7
PUBLISHED BY PUBLISHAMERICA, LLLP
www.publishamerica.com
Baltimore

Printed in the United States of America

Acknowledgments

I never would have believed that I could ever write a book such as this. The Lord has brought me through a terrific journey thus far as the senior pastor of a small church on the outskirts of Ventura, California. This journey has taught me so much and has been so unbelievably incredible that I felt it necessary to share.

It is with the Lord's guidance that I put the words to paper. I would like to thank God for my wife of 17 years, Terri, and our children, Cassie (16) and Matthew (7), who have been so supportive throughout all that has happened in our lives. I cannot thank the people of First Baptist Church or Casitas Springs enough for their continued support. They have followed this humble servant through the fire.

I thank Pastors Ken and Denise Drake (Hilo, Hawaii), Dale and Joy Roberts (Phelan, California), and Mike Moore (Oak View, California) for their counsel in times of need and their unwavering support of my ministry. May God truly bless all those mentioned.

They seemingly came out of nowhere. I was preparing to leave the church driveway, which doubled as the parsonage driveway, when they surrounded my car. I previously had some conflict with these young men and women as the pastor of the first Baptist Church in Casitas Springs, California.

The leader placed himself squarely between my station wagon and the street. They all began yelling in unison. "Get out of town! We will not take this any more!" I looked at the leader and began to concentrate on him alone. I asked him if we could pray together, which he promptly refused. I could hear the others getting more and more riled up as they began to shout louder and louder. By this time my wife and the women who were with her in the house began to notice the commotion.

One woman began to shout support for my efforts–"I've got your back, pastor," she said.

I focused once again on the leader of this pack of neo-Nazi skinheads. I told him that I would pray with him, and then I began to move toward him.

His response was full of rage. "If you come near me, we will kill your wife and kids and burn this church down. We were here before the church! You've got to leave town!"

It wasn't until then that I realized what he was trying to say to me. Up to this point I had thought it was a bunch of young people who were upset at my involvement in the community. At that moment I understood that it was Satan himself–more specifically his demons–that were speaking. I knew the leader, at 26, was the oldest, and the rest ranged from 15 to 21 years of age. If this was the truth, then they were not here before the church since the church had been established in 1950, over 48 years prior.

As I stood and faced them in the street, I realized one thing: MY calling into the ministry was God's to give–had I known anything about the "physical" danger of ministering in a small town in California, I might never

5

have answered God's call.

I spoke to the leader saying, "I know who you are–and I rebuke you in the name of Jesus. Be gone!" and miraculously, they disappeared by running in three different directions! *WOW!* I thought. *God really does provide for our protection.* After they had gone, almost as if by divine plan, the sheriff's department showed up to control the event. Little did they know that God was already in control.

The Beginning

The event I just told you about is one of many that have filled the last six-and-a-half years of my life as senior pastor of this small church in a volatile community. I want to stress that it wasn't the events themselves that prompted the writing of this book, but the power behind the miracles that came from these events. Those very young people who came to attack my family and me that day would one day be present in the church to hear the gospel message preached from my lips. They would even come to understand that there were powers far greater than the power they served working in this small town. They would go so far as to approach me at my home and ask forgiveness for the vandalism and threats and offer a financial donation for the inconvenience.

God began a work in me that day in October. He began to show me that the scripture was more real than I could have ever imagined. The Bible tells us:

> Believe me when I say that I am in the Father and the Father is in me; or at least believe in the evidence of the miracles themselves. I tell you the truth, anyone who has faith in me will do what I have been doing. He will do even greater things than these, because I am going to the Father. And I will do whatever you ask in my name, so that the Son may bring glory to the Father. You may ask me for anything in my name, and I will do it.
>
> (John 14:11-14 NIV)

I was naïve enough to believe that Jesus meant what he had said that day long ago. I believed in the miracle I had witnessed that particular day; therefore, I believed that I was capable of doing even greater things than Jesus had done. This, to me, was a novel concept. This meant that the vision God had given me for this community could be real–this entire town COULD come to know Jesus as Lord and Savior. Where to start? That was the question of the day.

I began by preparing the church for the battle they had never fought; the battle against Satan. I read God's word feverishly and saw how the nation of Israel had to prepare for spiritual battle by first preparing themselves to listen to their God. Therefore, I began a Bible study in the Book of Acts, starting from the beginning and reaching into the very intestines of the early church. Why had they grown spiritually so quickly? What I soon began to realize is that our church had been sick and dying for a long time. It needed to be revived; but how?

My answer came through prayer. The church needed to deal with its sin. I, as leader, needed to allow the power of the Holy Spirit to work through me, which meant I had to get out of the way of the work of the Lord. This would require much work within my inner being and within the congregation.

The Church

What I have not told you up to this point is that the church had a reputation–a reputation for killing ministry and driving pastors away. There were only thirteen members in the church when I began, two of whom were members of the community. When I arrived in view of a call to the ministry here, the church literally broke down and almost self-destructed in front of my eyes. As I was preparing to preach the evening message, the quartet of church members were singing a special song designed for the occasion. In the middle of this song one member (a woman) began yelling at some rowdy teenagers in the back of the church. These teenagers happened to be the children of the lady playing the piano. This caused some grief and the piano player began playing as if she were beating on the drums. The children became more rowdy and hurled profanities and hand gestures in the quartet member's direction. What was so special about this moment was that the other three quartet members never missed a beat or failed to hit a note. It appeared as if this was commonplace for the church. As I left that evening to drive back to the university I was attending, I asked my wife why the Lord wanted us to minister here. In disbelief she said, "I don't know, but He does."

As I arrived on this mission field, it didn't take me long to figure out that the church had not been performing its called mission within the community. The community had no respect for the church and the church members were too concerned with the minor details of "doing church" to notice that God had called them to minister to those around them. It wasn't always like this, but as is often the case, Satan had drawn the people into a state of apathy where they had become lost. Things needed to change! And it was on that day in

October 1998 that they began changing. I began to teach about the first church as I simultaneously began to search for the very physical representation of the Holy Spirit in my life. I wanted to see!

+++++

The Book of Acts begins with the inhabitation of the Holy Spirit within the very leadership of the church. The disciples present on the day of Pentecost were literally transformed from fishermen and farmers, tax collectors and citizens into the machinery that would preach, teach, and live the Gospel of Jesus Christ. I noticed, as if for the very first time, that leadership focused on the preaching, teaching and praying for the people while the daily details were left to others. It was this "system" of reaching out that furthered the kingdom of God and brought thousands in one day and many in the years to come, to the realization that Jesus is Lord.

Later that month, I preached on the prayer Daniel offered up to God in repentance for the sins of his forefathers and the nation as a whole. I read that prayer to the congregation and then reread it to the Lord in front of them, inserting our church name wherever the nation of Israel was mentioned. I pointed out that the church of old, the church of apathy, was going to have to repent and change. I told the congregation that day that if they wanted to see where Satan was working, they should "look beside you, you invited him in here with you today."

That one statement brought forth much conversation over the next few weeks–or could it have been that as I made that very statement the whole church became dark (in the middle of a sunny morning) and, as it was later stated by many, the only thing that was visible of me was my very white shirt.

Now I am not so naïve as to believe that an inflammatory statement such as the one I made that Sunday wouldn't cause some commotion and might result in my dismissal from this church. However, if I believed what I had read in God's word, and if I had survived the attacks of the enemy to this point, then I must have confidence that the Lord would work out the details, especially since he had given me the message to bring.

It wasn't long after that Sunday that I was again challenged by the youth in the neighborhood. As I was preparing for a Sunday evening service, I noticed that there was a growing crowd of hostile young people gathering at the front of the church. As I approached them, they moved into the yard of the neighbor next door. I asked if there was anything that I could do for them and one said, "Can you outrun a nine?" He said this rather softly while moving his left hand to his belt region.

I couldn't believe what I was hearing. I said, "I am so fat that I can't outrun my shadow. What makes you think I can outrun a nine millimeter?" After saying this, I slowly turned around, walked toward our streetwise deacon, and said, "I think I was just threatened with a gun."

The deacon went and stood in the middle of the crowd and asked which one had the audacity to disrespect his pastor. He challenged them to come after him. I realized that this deacon, although he had the right heart, was bringing the wrong message; these young people needed to be loved, not abused, into the kingdom.

The Work Begins

My search for the right technique in dealing with an apathetic, poorly trained spiritual force, began in the Bible. I went in search of evidence of the Holy Spirit's work within the church. It seemed to me that whenever the people prayed and were OBEDIENT, the Lord blessed them. I also noticed that as they became more and more obedient, their faith grew stronger and stronger. We needed that! We needed a faith that would bring down the powers that ruled this community and had infected the church. I began to pray daily, asking the Lord to show me what, in me, needed to change in order to allow His power to flow through me as it did in the leaders of the first century. I was led through a series of scriptures that, suffice it to say, brought me to a better understanding of MY responsibility in my relationship with God, and the power that came through obedience. I then went in search of a stronger faith.

What was interesting about this journey is that I had been on a similar journey while attending California Baptist University (College at the time). I asked many pastors, professors and Christians alike one question: "When we say that someone doesn't have enough faith, what does this mean? What is enough faith?" To a person, I received that standard biblically based response, "Faith is the evidence of things hoped for but not seen." Great! But what did this mean? It wasn't until I began my personal search as a senior pastor that I figured it out. Faith is this: Going one step beyond what you yourself can do. It didn't matter if I was preaching, teaching or encouraging, if I went one step beyond my words, my abilities, my understanding, then it was the Lord who would be doing the work, and THAT was faith.

I couldn't face the onslaught of attempted physical violence, the years of spiritual persecution, the emotional roller coaster that came with ministry in this church without the faith the Lord provided each time I allowed Him to do the work–that is, each time I stepped out of my own way.

+++++

In my attempt to rid myself of the walls I had built up between my Lord and me, I thought it best to address my issues with "gifts." I first felt that I needed to understand what this "speaking in tongues" meant that accompanied the inhabitation of the Holy Spirit as stated often in the Book of Acts. It seemed that when there was prayer, obedience, and repentance, the people were gifted with the ability to speak in tongues. I was "trained" by the Southern Baptists, and we didn't believe in the speaking in tongues or the fact that these spiritual gifts still were available in today's Christianity. I was fearful that I would turn into a Pentecostal preacher if the Lord ever revealed that the gifts still existed. But then again, I could not work within the framework of John 14 without believing that I too would be able to see healing and other miracles as performed by Jesus.

The dilemma continued until one day when I heard from the Lord at a local Baptist pastors' breakfast. I was praying for my close friend and Christian brother for healing. I was praying audibly in front of the other pastors when I began to pray in tongues. I quickly clamped my hand over my mouth and waited a few minutes before I resumed the prayer. When I began again, I spoke in tongues again. I continued until I was done, got up, paid my bill, and left. A fellow pastor came out and, through his laughter, asked me if I understood what had just happened. I told him that I had been on a three-month search (at that point) for the truth about tongues and I had received my answer. I would like to say to all my fellow Southern Baptist pastors that I cannot control my prayer language, meaning I can't conjure it up, and when I pray, I feel I have communed with the very essence of God himself. God blessed me that day and has continued to since then.

I was learning to trust the Lord in his leading in spite of denominational interpretation, and I don't single out the Southern Baptists here, either. Denominations are, by definition, separated by interpretation of scripture. I reread that scripture which caused me conflict and arrived at the following: God still provides his gifts for the purpose of building his kingdom to glorify himself.

+++++

I felt that if God still gifted His people in this manner, then healing must also be a part of the picture. I took hold of the church's rather long list of prayer requests and asked the members how long the prayer requests had been on the list. Some had been there for years without results. I asked them if they thought that their prayers could bring about the healing and answers to these requests. Some, unbelievably, actually thought that, though they were dutiful in prayer, some of the prayers were meant to stay on the list. I began to teach that our prayers were powerful, but only if we were obedient in our personal relationship with the Lord. We began purposefully praying for those on the list by gathering each Monday night and praying within the church walls. This eventually developed into a 24-hour time of prayer that still exists to this day. Slowly, we began to hear back from people that their prayers were being answered. Go figure! I could not have been happier! The Lord was beginning to show His people that He was still on the throne and they were beginning to believe it. However, there is the down-side of God's glory being revealed to His people–those who still won't believe.

Now I expected to receive opposition from Satan in the form of those who are unsaved and live as part of the world. I expected the physical threats from the neo-Nazi group in town, but I never expected to get such grief from within the leadership of the church.

Not long after arriving, as I began to make the necessary changes within the church as directed by God, leadership began to realize that they would no longer be in control of the minor details. This fear of loss of control drove the deacon leadership to come against me in an attempt to control my behavior. I resisted, and they left. I suppose I could go into detail, but anyone who reads this book will understand that often, within church, the lay leadership and deacon leadership run the pastor. God had given me explicit instructions: The call to this church was His to give and His alone to take away. I told the church members that I may not know how to "run" church, but I did know how to "listen" to God. It was then that I was informed that they, the deacons, were responsible for me being there; therefore I should be beholden to them for this job. I quickly informed them that this call was HIS.

After this minor altercation, things began to move quickly. The Lord directed me to lead the church through a time of repentance. We were instructed to identify the problems within the church and our own lives and ask the Lord for forgiveness. This played out in a visible fashion around the New Year. I asked the members of the church to write their most private sins on a piece of paper, and as the nation Israel had done, we approached a lit fire in the middle of the parking lot, and placed our sins on the fire (as a sacrifice) to show our desire to rid ourselves and our households of that sin. This began the year of repentance.

Working on repentance, while under attack from the community and from within the church, brought me to a better understanding of God's mercy and patience. I began to notice that people who were struggling the most had the worst attitudes about worship and church work. God also led me to his word: "Since then you have been raised with Christ, set your hearts on things above, where Christ is seated at the right hand of God. Set your minds on things above, not on earthly things." (Col 3:1-2 NIV)

This meant that those who came against us had their spiritual eyes out of focus. I relied on an old adage to help me here as well: "There, but for the grace of God, go I."

If I had not had my spiritual eyes focused on the Lord, I too would have had such an attitude about worship and church. I began to see around the attitude to the spiritual void behind the people and saw the enemy that controlled their behavior. As I understood it, you could not be in God's will and the enemy's will at the same time. This meant that when someone came against me personally in an aggressive manner, they were obviously following the enemy because God's word says that when we are in his will, we won't act in this manner. I can't tell you how many hurt feelings and aggravating arguments this has prevented.

Having the knowledge and understanding of God's grace and the patience and mercy to accompany it, helps when one is faced with a challenge from within the church. One such challenge came when the enemy decided that I wasn't going to be scared off by the local gangs after they had come to apologize for their behavior. There was one last effort to unhinge my resolve to remain in this community church. As I was closing up the church one Sunday evening after worship, car lights from the last departing member focused on a group of young people standing across the street from the church. Each young person, thirteen in all, possessed an instrument to use in my beating; some had sticks of wood, some bats, and still others had metal poles. The member stopped his car, and together we stood facing the young people as I challenged their desire to hurt me. They left without incident.

The attack from within the church came as two members decided that I wasn't following God's will with regards to worship. Funny thing–they were both on the worship team at the time. Pride, when given a willing ear, can work to destroy the church's ministry faster than anything I have ever seen. What happened in our church happens in churches around the world. People begin to believe that their abilities exist because of hard work and not because God has chosen to gift them.

One such man had become the treasurer of the church and had effectively, through much maneuvering, relieved me from any responsibilities involving the finances of the church. I tell you this because it was on this point that he attempted to have me removed from the church. The man had become a friend to my family and myself. At the time, he had endeared himself to my young son. His involvement in my son's life was deep and complete. This fact made it much more difficult to accept what the enemy was trying to do through him and his cohort. The enemy knew that he couldn't stop the advance within the community, so he attempted to gain control of the church God was using to make the advances.

This man riled up his cohort to such a degree that he was able to bring, what is affectionately known in our church as the "Matthew 18," against me. I spent the entire day awaiting his arrival on my face before the Lord in the middle of the church. I didn't ask God to take this attack from me, but I did ask that he would give me the words necessary to encourage this man and woman. I asked that He give me the ability to show mercy and understanding toward these two.

The room was small and filled with many witnesses. I had the associate pastor there to represent fairness as the two brought their charges of financial impropriety against me. They had filled the room with those who were sympathetic to their cause (getting rid of me). Many of these witnesses were not regular attendees of the church, nor were they involved in the church ministry at the time. What they never expected was for me to be as peaceful as I was; I never expected the peace that I felt inside to be there, either. The Lord provided a grace that surpassed anything I could have done on my own. I was able to meet their challenge and face their wrath as they unloaded what seemed like two cannons at my integrity. With joy, I expressed a victory for the Lord as I left that meeting. This joy would be short-lived as they plotted to ambush the next Sunday's service with a complaint brought before the church in an attempt to "church" me.

Once again, I went to the Lord in prostrate fashion before the altar in the church. I asked the Lord to guide and direct my actions, fully aware that I would have to get out of the way in order for Him to do His work.

I preached that Sunday and noted that these two arrived late to present their findings to the church body as a whole. I gave them that opportunity by retiring to the parsonage. My understanding of the event is this: They brought their cause; they yelled their objections and left without satisfaction. The Lord prevailed again! As if I could doubt. However, the enemy wasn't satisfied with that. The man called as many church members as he could think of to let them know that "in no uncertain terms," if the pastor wasn't fired, he and his guitar wouldn't be back. They told him to enjoy his new church. Again, not the right response, but these kinds of reactions would soon change.

I believe that it was my faith and belief in God's power that allowed me to see beyond these two individuals to the enemy who controlled them. I now preach to the congregation that the one way to get past the reality that faces us in the form of very real physical or emotional danger is to look beyond the person in front of you to the force behind their actions. As a church, we have begun to see the potential in every person brought into our midst, allowing us to look beyond their spiritual condition of the present.

Time to Heal

The year following repentance was called the year of reconciliation. The Lord led me through a period of self-discovery that helped me to understand that my personal responsibility to Him required that I not only repent, but that I reconcile with those I have wronged. In doing this with my personal life, I realized that the church would not be able to grow spiritually unless it dealt with past sins through reconciliation.

We prepared to reach into the past and identify the sins of the church. I approached those who had been here for some time and asked for the details of the church as it had dealt with former pastors, people, leaders, and community members. They began to reveal a past filled with prejudice against the unclean, dishonor toward God's called leaders, and general ungodly behavior. We wrote down names, took down details and began the plan for reconciliation. This plan involved getting in touch with the former pastors, leaders, community members, et cetera. We scheduled the reconciliation service for a June Sunday. To our surprise, very few showed to receive a public apology from the church.

However, God gets the glory through this year of reconciliation though few showed to participate in the actual service. It seemed that the church had so distressed a former pastor, causing him such great grief that not only did he leave the church, he left the ministry. He had not set foot into a church since leaving Casitas Springs. I contacted this pastor in his new profession as a chef and asked him to attend the service. I told him that I was particularly disturbed by the way the church had treated him. They had refused to pay him if he didn't do what they wanted, thereby handcuffing his spiritual hands and causing his family to be unable to buy food. This effectively drove him from the church.

What was surprising about this is how matter-of-fact the people were when they talked of what they had done. The enemy had so infested the church that, to this point, they were still unable to accept responsibility or express appropriate remorse. This attitude would change throughout this service and the years since then.

The former pastor was unable to make it to the service but he accepted my personal phone call and the apology offered and gave the most desired response, "I forgive you." The miracle in this is that the man went back to church the next Sunday and thereby back into the arms of his Lord and Savior, and not four months later, he died of a brain tumor. We had been instrumental in bringing him back to the church and fellowship and back to the Lord before he went to be with his savior for eternity. The church was beginning to heal.

+++++

As for my personal life, I was able to reconcile with my father and family. I had been in a long emotional battle with my father from an early age. This battle had fostered resentment and anger directed toward him. I publicly asked forgiveness for my lifelong anger toward my father while he was attending one of our services. I believe God used this moment to instruct the church as to how to go about asking for forgiveness and helped them to understand that this act of humility was not so difficult to perform.

It was also because of this year of reconciliation that I was able to forgive the man and woman who had previously come against me. I became painfully aware of the meaning of 1 Peter 13-16 which states, "Therefore, prepare your minds for action; be self-controlled; set your hope fully on the grace to be given you when Jesus Christ is revealed. As obedient children, do not conform to the evil desires you had when you lived in ignorance. But just as he who called you is holy, so be holy in all you do; for it is written: Be holy, because I am holy." (NIV)

This scripture tells me that I must ready my mind for battle (gird up the loins of your mind–KJV). I was to remember how I had acted when I didn't understand God's grace and the power of His Holy Spirit. He showed me how His spirit leads us to show grace toward others. I was no longer allowed to conform to the old ways of thinking; and if I couldn't conform, the church couldn't conform. We had not only to speak forgiveness, but act it out through visible reconciliation and thereby restoration. It was this year of reconciliation that led me to understand that once reconciled, relationships must also be restored.

A Godly Return

Restoration is referred to often in the Bible. The nation of Israel would become disobedient, and when they wouldn't listen, God would send them into exile or cause great harm to come to them in their own land. He would withdraw himself from their presence or punish them in a harsh manner. This is true for our relationship with God. If we are disobedient and rebellious then God often gives us a desert experience to recover from the foolishness. Should we still fail to recover, we are often left to our own desires (worldly) and given time to wander aimlessly without His direction. We are overcome by evil.

As I witnessed the ugly, old behavior disappear, I began to realize that our church needed to be restored to the Lord. We began a time of praising Him and seeking Him in earnest. During this time, I noticed that the people were unwilling to encourage each other because it left them open to ridicule if they were to divulge their sin. I liken it to a valley. We all will wind up walking down into the valley of sin at one point in our lives. However, we will walk as if we don't see others walking in that same valley. In fact, we will believe that if we stand still long enough, then the others will pass us by without noticing we are there. It is almost as if we are trying to blend in with the surroundings so that we won't have to admit that we are still in sin. It took some time, but we eventually felt comfortable enough to risk open judgment and we began, as a church, to support each other and pray over the sin in our lives as a congregation.

We gave up personal sin, prayed for each other, began to reach out into the community and slowly began to realize our own responsibility in our relationship, as a church body, to God. It was during this time that the church saw its greatest numerical growth. We went from 20 to over 100 in service. We began to reach out to those around us and saw 23 baptisms during this period. God began to use his people in this small community church in a powerful way.

It was such a powerful expression of God's love that the local newspaper took notice. In my attempt to be obedient to the Lord and to help the church restore its relationship with the community, I began the habit of walking through the neighborhood and praying for people's homes and families. I would walk in my flannel shirt and sandals, carrying a wooden stick to beat off dogs and roosters as I prayed for the community. I asked the Lord to show me where I lived–show me the spiritual community.

What He revealed was decay. It was as if the enemy had come into the community and spread out like a bad fungus. The enemy had enslaved the community. They were addicted to drugs, alcohol and abuse. I don't mean in small amounts; I am talking about widespread, deeply seated, generational addiction.

As I walked and prayed, it was revealed to me that there were eleven drug houses in the town, each visible to the naked eye. I began to pray for the removal of these houses and the enemy that possessed them. I don't mean that I wanted the people to leave, but I prayed against the powers behind the people. What happened is still talked about today within the community and the church. The houses began to be shut down, some by the police force, some through the evacuation of the people, and still some through the coming of the Lord into their lives. The town slowly began to see less and less of the police presence. The homeowners began to paint, renovate and clean up their homes and the newspaper discovered an angle–at least what it thought was an angle.

+++++

The Los Angeles Times, Ventura Edition, contacted me to see if I would be amenable to allowing them to come out and follow me on one of my prayer walks. I assured them that this would be fine, but they would have to get up pretty early in the morning to follow me around.

The next day they had someone at my home by 6:30 a.m. to accompany me with a camera. The woman who came followed me quietly and noticed that I would stop at particular houses and pray with hands raised, while I would simply pass by others. She began to question my methods. I told her that since I had been walking the community for some time, I had come to know the houses that had great family difficulty and where there was a need for God's presence. She asked me how I was able to discover this. I said, "Simple. Through God, and the mouths of those who live in the houses." You see; God had shown me that I had to meet the people in order to meet the need.

The woman asked if she could come out on a Sunday and photograph me in service. I was hesitant, but after talking with leadership, I allowed this to happen. This woman came and talked with the people, heard the excitement about what God was doing, and went to her newspaper to ask a reporter to do the story. Not one week later, a reporter and several pastor friends accompanied me as I went to the highest point in the town to pray blessings over the community. It was on this walk that the reporter got to see firsthand the work of the power of the Lord through his servants. As we walked to our destination above the town, we passed by some people, known to me, who were having difficulty starting their car. They told us that they had been working on it for several hours and were about to miss a very important opportunity to work. Knowing that these people needed the money, I asked if I might pray for them. They agreed. I prayed, and we went on our way.

At the top of the hill, our group stopped to pray over the community. We prayed prosperity and blessings, while binding the demonic influences. The reporter asked me a question that led me to believe that the newspaper thought it had stumbled upon an "angle" for my prayer walking. She quietly leaned over as others were praying and said, "you just want these people to come to your church."

I was quick to inform her that if all of these people came to know Christ as their savior today, they wouldn't all fit in the church. I said, "We wouldn't be able to meet their needs or minister to them. My desire is that they know Christ; where they go to worship is up to God, not me."

The look on her face was priceless. That look intensified when we passed by the people having trouble with their car and they informed us that it started not five minutes after I finished praying for them. I was sure to point out that God gets the glory, not I.

As if she didn't understand or believe, the reporter went through the neighborhood asking the people for their opinions of the church and its pastor. One man gave his summation of my presence in few words: "Since he arrived, crime has gone down." The town recognized, on one level, that there was change, even though they couldn't put their finger on the reason. However, it was evident that what I had been doing, and what the church had been doing, was having an effect. We were being restored by the Lord to the ministry in this community.

A Change Within

Not only had God begun to use his people in a powerful way to effect change within the community, but we began to see His work in our midst as well. There were people healed of diseases.

For instance, we began praying for an elderly woman within the congregation who suffered from lung cancer. We began by asking that God would confound the doctors during surgery to remove the tumors from her lung. We specifically asked that they would come out of the operating room scratching their heads. I asked with such specificity because the family was of little faith and needed confirmation that the Lord was at work here.

We waited only a short time for the surgeons to appear. They walked into our midst scratching their heads without explanation as to why they couldn't find the actual tumors that the x-ray had shown. This woman was to have her whole lung removed, but the doctors settled for a small portion instead. God is powerful!

In another instance, I was able to pray with a local man who suffered from alcoholism and I watched him stop drinking in one day. This man was so moved by this experience that, several years later, he called me once again.

"Pastor Bill," he began, "your church is known for having their prayers answered. I have a request. My father is in the hospital and they have called all of our family to be there with him because he has a serious brain aneurysm. He can't walk and is in the CCU. Could you please go and pray for him?"

I immediately dropped what I was doing, called a fellow pastor to go with me, and rushed to the hospital to pray for his father. When I arrived, I placed my hands on the man's head and prayed that the Lord would instantly and miraculously heal him. I noticed that during the prayer, my hands heated up and almost burned the man's brow; he noticed as well and spoke of it after I was finished. I was not surprised when the family called me later to inform me that the father was to be released the next day because the test given after I had prayed showed that the aneurysm no longer existed. God is the great healer. It is by His power that we, as servants, are able to accomplish His will.

Perhaps the most powerful display of God's mercy, grace, and power came in the county lock-up. I met Danny shortly after I first arrived at the church. I was making my rounds in the appropriate fashion on visitation night. He was seated in his garage on the avenue (known for drugs and other nefarious activity) having just completed smoking his drugs (speed). Our meeting was short and sweet. He didn't care that I existed and wasn't ready to come back to church. He had visited some time earlier, which was how we had gotten his name. Now, however, it was time for me to minister to him.

I can remember Danny asking me on one occasion as he visited our church how he could become a deacon. I could not believe this because he couldn't even take care of himself, let alone his family. He was a drug user on probation, welfare, and cash aide. He wasn't able to provide for his family of six, yet he wanted to become a deacon in the church. I was dumbfounded! What possessed people like Danny to believe that God would allow his leaders to live the life that he was living? It was then that I decided to pray daily for Danny and his family.

Eventually, I had the opportunity to visit with him in jail. He and I were the only people on the line that day. There were no other inmates or visitors talking at the time I visited with him. The jailers stood in a tower in the middle of a circle of jail cells three stories high. Danny was given permission to meet with me and he asked me through the plexiglass, "What am I going to do? I will probably be going away for a long time?"

I believed that he was scared of leaving his family for such a long time. Aahh! The perfect opportunity to bring the message. I told him to submit to the Lord's will for his life and to accept that he could not be the same person any more. I asked him if he was saved. He said he was, yet he also confided in me that he was looking for the same "feeling" he had when he first accepted Christ. I told him that acceptance is not only a feeling, but that it meant we were to be obedient to God's will.

He asked that I pray for him as he put his hand to the glass. I placed my hand on my side of the glass and began to ask the Lord to send his Holy Spirit upon Danny to make a change in his life. As I live and breathe–I watched the Holy Spirit come down upon Danny in the form of light, and I knew he would be changed forever! I was not the only person who saw the light that day. Those jailers buzzed in and asked Danny to turn the light off; they were informed that the light was not on.

Danny left jail soon after and quit welfare, went to driving school, got a job, began paying rent, moved, latched onto Jesus, achieved success in getting his felony record expunged, and at the time of the writing of this book, serves as the chairman of the deacons of FBC Casitas Springs. Isn't God wonderful?!

+++++

I began to see more and more of the Lord's miracles taking place within the church body. The people were realigning themselves with the Lord's will. This didn't eliminate all the struggles that they were having, but it showed them that it was possible to live in the Lord's will and be blessed. Miracles were happening every week. Now, I know that many might discount what happened and say that the Lord is not in the miracle business in the 21st century, but our church lived it. We experienced a time when the Lord provided money, cures from health issues, jobs, peace where there was no peace, and reconciliation where there was no reconciliation. To us, these were miracles. It took the power of the Holy Spirit to accomplish what transpired during those days in our church and community.

All the while the Lord was working through us, the enemy was plotting our demise. The community attacks were less frequent but the attacks to the people within the church began to increase. One of our deacons had to step down because of sexual immorality; he then had to step down as worship leader and finally as youth director. This process of accountability took a period of six years as the Lord showed him grace, through me, and then counted him punishable for the offenses. He still attends our service today and is beginning the process of restoration, having achieved success in the areas needed.

During this period in our church, I became more aware of how the enemy works in our lives. I personally was under great conviction to be more devoted to the Lord's will for my life. I began to change how I dealt with my wife and children at home. I also began to change how I reacted to, and dealt with, the people's personal struggles within the congregation. I believe that since the Lord was being victorious in many aspects of my life, and the life of the church, I was attacked in a different fashion–attacked with an old fear: cancer.

When my wife, Terri, and I were first married, we were happy, like most any other couple. That happiness was short-lived as we found out two months after we were married that I suffered from a brain tumor. The brain tumor had so affected me that my personality was changing and the pressure within my head caused great physical discomfort. We had always planned to have children, but the doctors indicated that we would not be able to conceive a child once I began the cancer treatments. Not being Christian at the time, and having no concept of faith, we made sure she was pregnant before I began treatment. This process took two months. I spent 18 months on treatments, saw many doctors and surgeons, and was about to go in for surgery when I asked my doctor to postpone it for three months. I was hoping that the new medicine would shrink the tumor, which had grown to the size of a golf ball and had by then ruined my vision.

During the three-month wait, my sister and her family invited me to a church revival. It was there that I received the knowledge that Jesus had died for me. Terri and I returned home the first night and asked forgiveness, praying to receive Jesus as our Lord and Savior. We were baptized two days later and began our church journey.

That Thursday following our baptism I was scheduled for my three-month MRI in preparation for the surgery. I went to the local MRI center and waited through the 90-minute exam for the technicians to tell me that the tumor couldn't be seen. My doctor became very angry and asked that they take another test. I endured another 90-minute exam only to arrive at the same conclusion–the tumor was gone!

I can remember with such clarity what the doctor said when I gave him my testimony of salvation, "Don't give me any of that faith crap. You will need to remain on this medication for the rest of your life." I stopped the medication

30 days later and was cleared of cancer within five years.

The blessing of this healing doesn't stop there. The doctors had informed my wife and me earlier that we would never be able to conceive a child after the treatment for the tumor. However, much to our surprise, Matthew James joined our family eight years after Cassie was born, and three years after I was pronounced completely healed of cancer.

Now we arrive at the fear I referred to earlier. Satan knew that I was fearful of dying a slow death from cancer. Since the brain tumor, I had several other tumors removed from my body. I was sure that I would never die of cancer; at least that is what I told my family and myself. It was during a time of joy and prosperity in the church that the enemy struck again.

I was sitting at the kitchen table in my home when I felt a pain in my side that surpasses all other pain I have ever felt, even that of the brain tumor. It literally felt as if I was being pierced in my side by a long sword. I went to the emergency room for medication, and later to the doctor for diagnosis. It was determined that I had gallstones, very large and very painful gallstones. I went into surgery a short time later to have my gallbladder removed. It was during this surgery that my surgeon, the best in the area, and a self-proclaimed genius, discovered that my gallstones were not stones at all, but a tumor. He told my father that the stones had metastasized into cancer and that they would have to biopsy the tumor to know more.

A week later, I still had not heard from the doctor as to the outcome of the biopsy. When I called on the Tuesday after the surgery, I was told that the lab had missed the biopsy and that they would complete it that day and call me with the results. I eagerly awaited the outcome. Meanwhile, my father and I went to the local Baptist pastors' breakfast and had them pray over me for a good outcome. One pastor, Ken Drake, the man I was praying for when the Lord blessed me with the gift of tongues, prayed that the tumor would be gone from the gall bladder even as it sat in that sterile lab.

Now this was too much! My father and I, with little faith, had some difficulty accepting that someone would pray for the gallbladder to be void of the tumor AFTER it had already been removed, identified by the doctor, and revealed to us. I knew that God could do anything, but there remained the doubt. Was I worthy of such a blessing? I called my doctor later that afternoon and after much coaxing, got him to respond to my call. He was reluctant to tell me the news. My father feared the worst, but I pushed him for the diagnosis. He said, "I don't know how to say this, but the tumor didn't exist. It was as if we took your gallbladder out for no reason."

I shouted for joy! God was victorious again! I couldn't help but think that I had to go through this physical attack to truly understand how powerful God truly is. The enemy was NOT going to get at me as long as I was present in God's will.

God Bestows Gifts

This period of personal struggle was also a time of discovery for me as well as many within the congregation. We learned that God's gifts were available to us today and began to see an increase in these gifts. One evening as my family and I sat down to dinner in the parsonage, there was a sudden change in the spiritual climate of our home. I became irritated with my children for no reason and began shouting at my wife when suddenly I realized that this was a spiritual attack. Now this doesn't excuse my behavior; I shouldn't have been aggravated. However, I did know enough about the enemy, and the Lord, to know that I needed to pray. In prayer, I was instructed to go outside and remove the demonic presence. As I left the house, I was completely surprised to find a local witch standing before my home with her hands raised, cursing us. I asked if I could help her. She said that she would like to sit with her cat, which was by her side. I told her that if she needed me I would be in my office in the church. I prayed against what she was doing and soon thereafter, she left.

I was curious as to what her reasoning might be for cursing our home, so when I got to my office I asked my wife to come out and see me. As she arrived in my office she said to me, "You do realize that there are demons on the roof of the house, don't you?"

I told her I did, and then took a second look and realized that she could see them. God had blessed her with the ability to discern spiritually! I was new to this so I called some other members of the church, and since it was Bible study night, I asked them to stop at the end of the driveway as they arrived and walk the property. As the people arrived they walked the property, and to a person, told me that something was wrong with my house. God had confirmed my wife's gift through the people of the church, even without their knowledge.

When the people were all present, we began the process of freeing our home of the presence of demonic spirits. There were several present who could feel and sense that there was something wrong with the house. One man, who was not a believer in spiritual attacks prior to coming that evening, began to pray around the back of the house and was stopped from advancing in prayer by what he referred to as a demon. I stood back and watched as several people placed their hands upon the outside walls of the house and began to pray. Each one quietly and secretly came to me and said that it felt as if the house was moving. I, like them, was a little confused, but believed that, with prayer, all would be set right once again. Needless to say, we won the battle that evening.

I suppose we could have then become a church that focused on the enemy and went demon hunting. I, however, was assured of one thing: God was the focus and the enemy was just a nuisance we faced when following God's will. There have since been many times we have walked the community and prayed for deliverance from oppression.

+++++

Deliverance from oppression sounds really "new age" if you ask me. I never looked at the Bible and thought of deliverance from evil as something other than delivering a person from demonic possession. Since fighting the spiritual battles in this church, however, I have arrived at a new understanding. Deliverance from drugs, alcohol, abuse and other sin is, to me, deliverance from evil. I have seen people quit drinking and using drugs. I have seen them be delivered from being slaves to the sin in their life just through simple prayer. We saw how the Lord used us to lift others up in prayer as a way of drawing us closer to Him and of freeing those whom we pray for from the oppression of the enemy.

On one such occasion, I was praying in a particularly drug-infested portion of our community. The road I walked led to the top of a hill that overlooked what is known as Edison Curve. This curve was part of the road that connected the four-lane freeway to the small two-lane road through our town. Many people had been killed in car accidents right at the point of this curve. I had already been praying for the curve as I drove through it going to and from town, but I felt I needed to investigate more. I went to the hill overlooking the street and saw something I never expected to see. As I prayed over the curve, the Lord revealed to me that this was the gateway to the Ojai Valley. This was where the enemy focused his power because it caused distraction for those attempting to serve the Lord in the valley.

I realize that many might find this disbelieving and had I not experienced it myself, I would feel the same way. However, the Ojai Valley is home to many new age religions. It is the center for "higher" enlightened thinking, witch activity and Scientology. We have many movie and television stars who live in Ojai that are members of the Scientology church. We have the Hell's Angels and other gang activity as well as Indian ritualistic behaviors. This valley was a stronghold of enemy activity and our town was right at the very entrance. I began to realize why God showed me the vision of total repentance and why the enemy wanted me to quit. This was a valuable piece of real estate for the enemy.

I prayed for God to close the gate and rebuked the enemy at all points. It was during this prayer that, and I kid you not, a large black dog jumped off a small hill to my right and tried to attack me. He literally flew off the hill with a growl. I normally would panic in this situation since I am terrified of dogs and spiders, but I only held up my hand and told the dog, while it was still in mid-flight, to "go away." It hit the ground and disappeared down the street with a yelp.

The Fruit of Obedience

The church God had sent me to was beginning to learn about the fruit of the spirit and the power of God in fighting the battles with the enemy. The "fruit of the Spirit is love, joy, peace, patience, kindness, goodness, faithfulness, gentleness and self-control." (Gal 5:22-23a NIV) We began to take on the characteristics of God through prayer and obedience to His will for our lives personally and for the life of the church. We were changing!

We saw people from the community begin to come to church. These were people with full-blown tattoos stating their affiliation with white pride in their past. They were raw, unclean, and in need of the Holy Spirit. They were needy and unable to give anything to the church upon their arrival. Where once the people of the church would require that they clean up their act before accepting them into God's house, these people were readily accepted and welcomed with open arms and the love of the Lord. The church grew so much that there was need to expand the fellowship hall for the favored pot luck luncheons. God's glory was everywhere and we were riding a year-long high in the Spirit, and then came the crash.

I began to think that I was invincible. I began to think that I was doing everything right. That is until I met the enemy face-to-face in familiar territory. The church was once again without finances and we were experiencing one of the greatest tests of our faith. We were being asked almost daily to help provide for someone within the community as well as pay the bills to keep the church open. My salary was often delayed to pay something else or to provide for others. I went before the Lord and asked for His help in speaking to the people. He told me to continue to encourage them to help others with as much as we could and to let the finances be His worry. Now, THAT was hard to communicate to those in leadership who continually worried about the little details, let alone something as big as this. All I can say is that we haven't closed our door yet, and we still help out many within the community. God has provided every time the church has had a need or a need comes to us from the community.

+++++

It was during this season in the life of the church that I began to work at a secular job. I was hired to write curriculum for a local distance learning school. I wrote course work for a school in Japan affiliated with the school I worked for in Ojai. It was here that I developed a relationship with the owners of the school in Ojai, and eventually I was hired as one of their teachers. This job provided the much-needed income for my family as well as, through tithing, the income for the church. What it also provided was an opportunity to see the Lord work in different ways, to learn more about His power as it is expressed through his people.

The school I was working for eventually fell on hard times. Their accountant had taken money and the school was in danger of closing its doors. I offered my services as an accountant (something I did prior to ministry) free of charge. I would help them recover and then go back to teaching. What I was given was the golden opportunity to pray for this business that was located in the middle of a city of evil. The company itself was imploding due to some personal ego struggles within. This destruction had to be stopped or many would lose their livelihood. I did all that I could do at the time: I prayed. I began to arrive early, pray over the building, bind the enemy, and ask God's blessing.

Within days, people focused on the struggle at hand and they began to work out differences. People who needed to leave, left. What is interesting, and here is where I see God's power, is that the replacements I hired were Christians. Now you must understand that nowhere on their application did they specify their belief in God, and it was not until after they were hired that they revealed themselves. This is God at work.

The company survived and has done well. When I left, the employees gathered around to see me off and expressed their sorrow at my leaving. They told me that I brought a peace to the office when I arrived. "Things seem happier with you here. Are you sure you have to go?" they asked. I have only recently given up the second income to be sure to devote 100% of my time to the Lord's work.

I was excited to see how the Lord was working through me. I began to praise Him in the worship services and out in the community. Our congregation became more active in reaching out and allowing God to use them in ways that seemed impossible before. We were a church on the move! We were determined to see the enemy pushed out of town and the Lord glorified while it happened.

When I first arrived, we began a yearly tradition of reaching out to the community by throwing a big block party in the church parking lot. The first event saw 36 people show up for free food, clothing, and entertainment. Our last block party boasted an outreach to over 365 people. This growth in outreach is a direct result of the recognition of God's power in our personal lives and within the congregation. The congregation took hold of the vision of years earlier and began to believe that God would use them, a poor beleaguered people, to build His kingdom.

+++++

I often refer back to the biblical story of Gideon. God took the smallest man in the least tribe and called him to lead a people into battle. When the Lord found Gideon, he was hiding in a cave threshing wheat. He was obviously terrified of the enemy. Our church had spent years hiding in the cave, terrified of being called into battle. Scripture pointed out that Gideon went into battle with what he thought was a large army, but God pared that army down. Gideon won the battle because although it looked like things were getting worse as the Lord pared down the fighting force, he was determined to be obedient. This story spoke volumes to me because in the midst of all this fighting, there were losses. People fell to sin, some left the church and others remained in the cave. We lost leaders and lay people to various spiritual injuries.

There were times when I became discouraged and thought that I was being of no use to God or these people. I, too, began to question the vision God had given me when I first arrived. I thought that these people were stubborn and should be left here to their own devices. I often beseeched the Lord and asked that He move me elsewhere. It was at these moments that He said no, by reminding me of the vision He had given me. It was also at these moments that He reminded me of the story of Gideon. If God could use the least of His nation to reveal His glory and His power, then He could use our church.

I am reminded of the story of Shadrach, Meshach, and Abednigo. They withstood the fiery furnace knowing that God was in control. If they were that confident in God's power and grace, then I, too, should be that confident. I asked three times in six years for permission to leave, and each time I was reminded of HIS call. Each time I was reminded that throughout His word He gives story upon story, and detail after detail, of how His glory and His will wins over all others. It has taken this long, but I now understand that I am called of GOD to reach out in a special manner (as a pastor) to a people lost and confused. I am called of HIM to shepherd His flock with care and obedience. I guess what I am trying to say is this: once I figured out that the call was His to give and His to take away, it was easier to remain in His will.

Victory

Now I move on to the two most powerful displays of God's power that have affected me in a most personal way. I begin with the man I talked about earlier, the man I was praying for when the Lord chose to reveal his gift of tongues, the man who prayed for the healing of my gallbladder–Ken Drake.

I met Ken when he appeared at one of the pastors' breakfast meetings shortly after my arrival. I knew very little about him except that he was suffering from a debilitating illness known a peripheral neuropathy. His nerves in his legs were literally deteriorating and causing an incredible amount of pain. This pain gradually grew worse and caused him to be laid up in a hospital bed on the first floor of his home.

I took it upon myself to pray for Ken because I had been healed, and therefore I knew that he could be healed. It was during one of these prayer sessions when the Lord revealed to me two things about Ken's future: (1) He was going to be healed and would give testimony at a local church and (2) His healing was for the church's benefit, not to be used for him alone. I quickly told Ken of my vision and promptly went in search of the church I had seen in that vision. I must have visited 30 churches in the time between vision and fulfillment.

When Ken and I went in search of the truth about his illness, we began with the inside. We prayed together in search of what Ken might have to do to align himself completely with God's will. Ken was led in prayer through a series of scriptures that allowed him to see areas in his life that needed immediate attention. It was a blessing to watch Ken's gradual transformation and as a result, the transformation of his family. There were many people around the world praying for this particular healing. At times, it seemed that the healing would never happen. Ken came to our church many times to receive relief from his pain. Our church property was anointed, and when he came to receive prayer for his body, he would leave with a reprieve from the pain. The congregation recognized that its obedience in prayer offered hope to those in pain, both physical and emotional.

God used me to help Ken endure the pain as he learned more and more about himself and his future ministry. It took many months to come to the understanding of the meaning of the words "your healing would be for the church." Prayers eventually revealed that God was showing the church that there would be pain, repentance, and healing, in that order. It was a call to the universal church to repent! There came a time when the pain got so bad that Ken became bedridden. In an attempt to prevent permanent disability, I went to dinner with him and his wife and, once outside, knelt before his wheelchair, laid my hands on his feet and legs, and began praying. I prayed that God would allow ME to receive the pain and swelling that he had in order that he might not be bedridden.

In the middle of this private and quiet prayer, I heard his wife exclaim, "Oh God, look at his hands!"

I opened my eyes, and as had happened many times before, my hands were swollen and Ken's feet and legs were not. Prior to this moment, I was the only one who knew that this would happen each time I prayed for Ken. This was the closest I have ever come to understanding unselfish love for another brother or the thought of giving my life for another. Ken and I remain the closest of friends to this day, and we are partners in a ministry to bless pastors located in Hawaii.

But what of his healing and the church testimony he was to give? Things got so bad for Ken that he actually thought of suicide. He was relegated to a bed in the lower floor of his home where he was fed and dressed each day. He was dying, and he knew it. It wasn't until a pastor from Guatemala came to visit that Ken's life changed. This pastor, profiled in the *Transformation* video, was on a speaking tour in our county. Our local missionary asked if he would be willing to visit a sick friend. The pastor said that he was here for this very purpose, so they joined Ken and his family at their home that afternoon. After twenty minutes of prayer, Ken was jumping, skipping, and running without any pain. The hospital bed was retired for good!

I was called immediately and asked to go to a church located in Ventura, California, to hear his testimony that night. I arrived at the church early, and as soon as I saw the inside, I realized that this was the church in the vision. I walked outside in tears to greet Ken and his family. They looked at me quizzically and I shook my head. "This is the one," I said. The Lord was given all the glory and the rejoicing was profound. However, the story doesn't end here. We had much to learn.

Our church rejoiced with Ken and his family and he came to give testimony as to what the church would go through in the coming years. We listened and braced for the coming time of pain and repentance. We began to think that all the struggles with Ken were over. However, during the season that followed, I was called upon several times to pray for Ken as he came under physical attack from the enemy. It was so sever at times that he was tossed about like a rag doll on his bed. I distinctly remember walking into his room and seeing his pastor and several family members in prayer around his bed as he was being flipped over and over, seemingly without touching the bed. I walked in, clapped my hands, and said, "Let's get this party started." I was assured of victory because through all the struggles at our church, through all the personal attacks of my physical body, through all the spiritual and emotional attacks, the enemy NEVER won the battle as long as I was faithful to listen to the Lord. Within fifteen minutes the party was over, and the Lord was victorious.

+++++

The second awesome display of God's power comes through personal tragedy. In September 2002, my wife came to me and stated that she no longer loved me and was thinking of moving out. The news was devastating and I was sent into a tailspin of slipping faith and grief. How could this happen? I was sure that I had done everything in our 15 years of marriage to make things work. We had some struggles, but nothing that would cause this drastic a situation. I thought that I was completely in the Lord's will. Things were progressing well at church and in my personal walk with the Lord. I never saw this attack coming. It was at this time that I took a profound

43

step toward the Lord. Over the next two years, I would completely submit every aspect of my life and being to the Lord. I realize that this sounds absurd. Giving our lives completely over to the Lord's will seems like an unattainable goal, but I was placed in a very precarious position: The church was likely to fire me, our children were going to suffer, and the enemy was sure to win this battle over my faith. I was broken in two. I was not sure my faith could withstand what was about to happen.

I spent the next three months talking with the children and trying in every possible manner to keep my wife at home. Despite all efforts, she left in January of the following year. The next step was to talk with the church. I had several leaders already praying for healing in our marriage, but now the time came to bare my very personal struggles before the church body as a whole. I considered all that I knew of pastors who had faced the same situation and was fully expecting the church to ask for my resignation. This was not to be the case. The church had learned something of God's power over the past four years in our journey together. The church knew God could fix this!

My wife moved 400 miles away and left the children to live with me. She began to build another life for herself over the next six months. From the moment she left, the church began to publicly pray for her return and healing. This prayer continues today as I write this book. Over the next few months, I began to settle on the fact that I was probably going to get divorced. However, I didn't give in to the idea until the Lord released me one day from the contract of marriage. I didn't fully understand why, but I no longer felt the deep grief I had previously. I was going to make it and the children would survive. It was time to file for a final separation.

Now I had received a message from the Lord, through vision, that Terri would be fine and would return to Him. Ken Drake had received the same vision and understanding from the Lord, as well. I was assured that she would be fine, but not assured that she and I would be fine as a couple.

I was leading a men's retreat at a local lake when I received that call from Terri stating that she had received the final paperwork for separation. She was in tears, struggling with the notion that she would only have visitation rights to the children and that our marriage would finally be over.

I explained to her that she could avoid all of this if she would seek therapy. We had tried in the months before she left, but she refused to accept what the therapist was saying. I told her that I would pay for the therapy if she decided to go. She did. In the middle of her therapy, she realized her destructive behavior of the last 15 years. She was diagnosed with borderline personality disorder and dissociative disorder due to trauma in her early childhood. She began to reestablish continual contact with me and eventually asked that she be able to return. I was in a quandary. I was sure that the Lord told me she would be healed, and I didn't want her back until that happened. As a matter of fact, I spent a night out in the middle of the parking lot of the church and yelled at the Lord for an hour, pleading with him not to bring her back until she was healed.

It was then that He reminded me of His word: "Submit yourselves, then, to God. Resist the devil, and he will flee from you. Come near to God and he will draw near to you... Humble yourselves before the Lord and he will lift you up." (James 4:7-10 NIV)

I had to submit fully to his will for my life, even if it included bringing someone back into my life who had caused me so much grief over 15 years and certainly great pain over the previous six months. I did as He instructed and the church, true to its teaching, gathered her back into the fold without reservation.

She began intense therapy here in town. Over the past two years, she has come to understand her past, her actions, her inner self and her God. She has been completely restored to leadership and as wife and mother. She leads the women's group and is instrumental in the writing of this book.

God was powerful in both Ken's and Terri's cases because we allowed Him to lead. Had I gone ahead of Him and tried to affect changes on my own, I would have failed miserably and God would never receive the glory.

+++++

The journey over the past six years as pastor of the First Baptist Church in Casitas Springs, California, has been an eventful one. I have learned more in this field of ministry than I could ever have learned at the university that taught me to read and understand the Bible. I am forever thankful to California Baptist University and the professors there for giving me the opportunity to learn God's word. However, nothing compares to actual battlefield experience to provide an education on the power of God.

Too often Christians get caught up in the process of "doing" church and miss the opportunities to reach out to others. I pray that, after reading this book, you are encouraged. I pray that these words are not wasted. God is powerful to bless us in all we do if, and only if, we remain in His will.

When I surrendered to the pastoral ministry in September 1994, I thought that I would be able to direct my ministry. I was sure that I would bring change to anyone to whom I preached. However, it took physical threats, internal church struggle, illness, and personal tragedy to prove to me that I had nothing to do with my calling to become a pastor. Whatever I have accomplished has been done in His name, and with his complete control.

I feel assured of one thing: He chose me. He equipped me. He leads me. He will protect me with His power. The call is His.

Printed in the United States
32536LVS00009B/421-453